Colbie Caillat
Breakthrough

Contents

This book was approved by Colbie Caillat

Arranged by John Nicholas

Cherry Lane Music Company
Director of Publications/Project Editor: Mark Phillips
Project Coordinator: Rebecca Skidmore

ISBN 978-1-60378-198-5

Visit our website at www.cherrylaneprint.com

Colbie Caillat: Breakthrough

Last time around, Colbie Caillat was feeling "Bubbly," and the entire pop world seemed to want a sip. But this time, effervescence flirts with explosiveness. For her sophomore album, *Breakthrough*, Colbie has shaken up her sound, bringing in a wider array of producers and players, and significantly picking up the tempo at times from her debut effort's signature ballads. So keep an eye on those carbonation levels: champagne corks may fly.

You'd be hard-pressed to consider an album as accomplished and successful as *Coco* an accident, yet that's almost what Caillat's 2007 freshman release was. The sudden mania it created at radio and retail "was a surprise for me," Caillat says, "because I hadn't really been in this business yet. I hadn't been doing shows. I wasn't trying to get signed. I just was this girl who wrote songs and put them up on MySpace." By the time Coco was released to stores, "Bubbly" was already

enough of an airplay sensation that the album debuted at No. 5. The massive success of a second single, "Realize," helped push the album to over two million shipments, in addition to almost six million individual digital tracks that were sold. "It all just happened naturally," says Caillat, "—and now I have to keep up with it."

The making of *Breakthrough* was far more purposeful than the ramshackle sessions that became Caillat's first album. Whatever might have been lost in the way of charming naiveté is more than made up for with greater experience and heightened maturity. "When I found out I had six months to make this album, it was so exciting because my favorite part is being in the studio and having a chance to get it right. "

"We tried different versions of a lot of the songs—some raw and acoustic; some with lots of harmonies and others with 20 more instruments than needed to be

there—just to see which version sounded best. We ended up having a lot of variety." But for all this diversification, there's at least one carry-over and constant: the front-and-center intimacy of Caillat's vocals, which fans already relate to coming through their ear buds like the voice of a warm and trusted friend.

Production credits for *Breakthrough* were split between two new helmers. One is hit-maker John Shanks, who's particularly known for his work with strong female artists like Kelly Clarkson, Sheryl Crow, Melissa Etheridge, Alanis Morissette, and the Wreckers. The other new guy behind the boards is Ken Caillat, most renowned for his work on one of the top-selling albums of all time, Fleetwood Mac's *Rumours*, and also, not insignificantly, for being Colbie's father. Bringing things full circle, the new album was recorded at Village Recorders in West L.A., where Ken Caillat met his future wife and Colbie's mother-to-be when

they were both working there during the making of Fleetwood Mac's *Tusk*.

Both John Shanks and Ken Caillat recorded basic tracks with a band playing live in the studio while Colbie sang along in the vocal booth. Beyond that similar approach to the early sessions, though, their approaches diverged. "My dad's recording is very organic and reveals the rawness and vulnerability in a song," she says. "And John Shanks is a great pop producer. His songs are perfect for radio."

"On this record, Caillat continues, "I was able to contribute a lot more of my production ideas into the recording. I had a better sense of how I know the songs should sound and feel, and what instruments should be added or taken away from them. Because I didn't get to do that on *Coco*, to really be able to make these songs completely my own was a special experience for me."

No one wanted to fix what wasn't broken about *Coco*, of course. At this time in music-business age, when new stars aren't even being added to the firmament anymore, Caillat's success was as close to overnight as it gets. Two years after its July 2007 release, the debut is still in the top 100, and stands as the 12th biggest selling digital album of all time. "Bubbly" is the 21st best selling digital track ever, with sales of more than 2.8 million, and was a No. 1 smash at Hot AC radio for 19 weeks and AC for 17. The music videos for the first album's songs were streamed over 22 million times. "Bubbly" was named Song of the Year at the last BMI Awards, and Colbie tied for Artist of the Year, for that song and "Realize." She was named the winner of *Billboard*'s Rising Star award, too, on top of nominations for the American Music Awards and Teen Choice Awards. If the bubble ain't broke, don't pop it, right?

Coming off such rare and covetable success, expanding the sonic palette beyond the mostly acoustic base of *Coco* for the new album wasn't undertaken lightly. "I didn't want to stray too far too fast from what my fans are used to from me," she says. "But I did want to grow and experiment and work with different people. I searched for the right balance."

Caillat expanded her circle of co-writers as well as producers, sitting down to work with hit crafter turned Idol maker Kara DioGuardi (who helped write three tracks, including "Begin Again") and Rick Nowels, who says, "I've worked with some really good writers—Madonna, Dido, Nelly Furtado, Jewel—and I'm just really impressed with Colbie's songwriting.

She's got her own voice and lyrical and melodic point of view; she's what I call a natural. And she's a proper singer-songwriter, which is a breath of fresh air today. I think everybody responds to strong songs sung emotionally, and everybody responds to *real*."

On *Breakthrough*, the emotional highs are higher, and the lows arguably lower. "All the songs are definitely about the rollercoaster of being in a relationship—happy, sad, breaking up, falling in love, just the whole cycle of it," she says. At the crest of this coaster, there's the first single, "Fallin' for You," which might be described as wearing its heart on its sleeve, if the tune's upbeat feel didn't conjure a kind of summer sleevelessness. "I had gone out on this 'friends' date and I realized I started liking him more than I thought I did," Caillat explains. "I was on cloud nine over this guy, thinking I was falling for him, so I wrote about everything we did hanging out the day before." Think "Bubbly" squared and gone to the beach.

But, in keeping with that coaster analogy, the album doesn't lack for romantic free-falls. "A lot of the songs from both *Coco* and the new album are about the same poor guy that I keep torturing in some way," she laughs. Knowing that he was more invested in the relationship than she was, she's written a number of songs from this boyfriend's point of view—including the hopeful "Realize" on the last album and the resigned but brave "Fearless" on this one. "The song 'Fearless' is sung by someone who's having their heart broken—but I really haven't been broken-hearted yet, so that song was me kind of switching it around from his perspective. I wrote it as him saying to me that he's fearless and this won't damage him for future relationships. The opening lines are 'If that's the way you love/You've got to learn so much.' And I really *do* have a lot to learn about love.

"All the songs have a different twist," Caillat continues. "It may not be exactly what happened to me, but it's happened in a situation that I've learned from or been watching. I wrote 'Breakin' at the Cracks' about one of my parents' friends who I've known my entire life. Everything in her life came crashing down on her at the same time: her mother died, her dogs died, then her father died, and finally her husband left her. I was on tour and my heart was hurting for her. So I started playing my guitar and crying while I was singing, imagining what it would take to get yourself out of that depression

and get your life back together. That was another song that had nothing to do with me, but I was expressing someone else's emotions, like I was sending a message to the world for them."

Having just been a fan herself until recently, Caillat thinks about how her most emotional songs will click with her own followers. "Because I know a Coldplay song like 'Fix You,' when I'm having a bad day, I can put it on and just pour my heart out—and then five minutes later, I'm ready for a smile again. So I want to have the perfect mixture of having those kinds of songs that you can cry to when you've had a horrible day and these upbeat, fun songs you can listen to at the beach or when you're driving."

Breakthrough's title track is another ruminative song about a friend's experience—in this case, that of Colbie's best pal, who has long been estranged from her father and continues to desperately desire a breakthrough in her relationship with him. But when Caillat applied the title to the album, it took on a different, more celebrative, strictly personal meaning.

"I'm 24, and I'm still trying to grow up as a woman and find out who I am and be comfortable in my own skin," she says. "I had gone through this very hard time where I was really down on myself, and I just kind of wanted to take the easy route and drop everything hard that was getting in my way. And I realized I had to step up and get past that. It took me a while, but I did finally break through my fears and insecurities. And that's why I felt that that would be a great album title, especially for my younger fans."

A newly minted star who's still discovering her boundaries, Caillat tries to stay open and even vulnerable. "You keep your guard up with some of the people that you meet. But I also think that fans should know who you are, and why be afraid of it? It's like that feeling you get when you see someone on YouTube with no makeup on or acting silly—whatever it is that you normally do—and it's like, 'Oh, they're doing it too, and it's okay; we can be who we are.' You just have to remind yourself not to hide what you do and who you are, because people like seeing that."

That's something Caillat clearly hasn't forgotten with this bigger, better, and even more intimate album. Finding out that increased amplitude and heightened transparency aren't mutually exclusive after all—that's the stuff that true bust-outs are made of. —July 2009

I Won't

Words and Music by
Colbie Caillat, Jason Reeves
and Makana Rowan

*Guitarists: Tune down one half step.

I won't do___ what you told___ me.___ I won't do___ what you said, no.___

I'm not gon - na stop feel - ing. I'm not gon - na for - get it.___

I don't want___ to start o - ver.___ I don't want___ to pre - tend___ that

you are not___ my lov - er, that you're on - ly my friend,___

To Codas I & II

7

friend. I won't.

Oh,

may-be you're not right for me.

May-be it's just hard to see.

Begin Again

Words and Music by
Colbie Caillat, Kara DioGuardi
and Jason Reeves

*Recorded a half step lower. (Guitarists: Place capo at 4th fret to play along with recording.)

You Got Me

Words and Music by
Colbie Caillat and John Shanks

Fallin' for You

Words and Music by
Colbie Caillat and Rick Nowels

Aadd2
Badd4
E5

I don't know what to do. I think I'm fall-in' for you. I've been wait-in' all my

Badd4/E
Aadd2
Badd4

life, and now I've found you. I don't know what to do. I think I'm fall-in' for you. _

E5
Badd4/E
Aadd2
To Coda

I'm fall-in' for you. _

Badd4
C#m

Oh, I just __ can't take __ it. __

26

Rainbow

Words and Music by
Colbie Caillat and Jason Reeves

Droplets

Words and Music by
Colbie Caillat and Jason Reeves

I'm leav - in' you. ___

I'm not sure if that's ___

I Never Told You

Words and Music by
Colbie Caillat, Kara DioGuardi
and Jason Reeves

Fearless

Words and Music by
Colbie Caillat, Kara DioGuardi,
Jason Reeves and Mikal Blue

*Recorded a half step higher.

the feel - ing, I'd still side with love.

And if I end up lone - ly, at least I will be

there know - ing I be - lieved in love.

Go on, go on and break

mp

dim.

Runnin' Around

Words and Music by
Colbie Caillat and Rick Nowels

*Play downstemmed notes 1st time only.

Repeat and fade

58

Break Through

Words and Music by
Colbie Caillat and Rick Nowels

May - be we just need - ed time. _____ Can we try _____ to let it go? _____ If we don't, _____ then we'll nev - er know. _____ I have tried _____ to break through, _____ but you know _____ that it's up to you. _____

It Stops Today

Words and Music by
Colbie Caillat and Jason Reeves

Breakin' at the Cracks

Words and Music by
Colbie Caillat and Jason Reeves

I think __ you took __ my heart __ a - way __
I know __ that I'll __ get through __ this.

when you said you're leav - in'. 'Cause right __ now, I __
I'm feel - in' strong - er some - how. __ I got __ my feet __

*Guitarists: Use open D tuning (low to high): D-A-D-F♯-A-D.
 Capo 1st fret (fret numbers next to chord diagrams indicate number of frets above capo).

I'm break - in' at ___ the ___ cracks, ___

and ev - 'ry - thing ___ goes

black. ___ It's an - oth -

er heart ___ at - tack, ___

and I ____ can't han - dle that. ____

1.
Woh, ____ love, ____ I ____ need ____ you back. ____

2. Woh, ____ love, ____ I ____ need ____ you back. ____

make it ___ last. ___

I'm

break-in' at ___ the cracks, _____

and ev-'ry-thing ___ goes black. ___

I need you back, _____ I need you back, _____

I need you back, _____

I need you back. _____